Thomson

by Iain Gray

Lang**Syne**
PUBLISHING
WRITING *to* REMEMBER

LangSyne

PUBLISHING

WRITING *to* REMEMBER

79 Main Street, Newtongrange,
Midlothian EH22 4NA
Tel: 0131 344 0414   Fax: 0845 075 6085
E-mail: info@lang-syne.co.uk
www.langsyneshop.co.uk

Design by Dorothy Meikle
Printed by Printwell Ltd
© Lang Syne Publishers Ltd 2017

ISBN 978-1-85217-119-3

Thomson

MOTTO:
Truth Will Prevail.

Echoes of a far distant past
can still be found in most names

Chapter one:

Origins of Scottish surnames

by George Forbes

It all began with the Normans.

For it was they who introduced surnames into common usage more than a thousand years ago, initially based on the title of their estates, local villages and chateaux in France to distinguish and identify these landholdings, usually acquired at the point of a bloodstained sword.

Such grand descriptions also helped enhance the prestige of these arrogant warlords and generally glorify their lofty positions high above the humble serfs slaving away below in the pecking order who only had single names, often with Biblical connotations as in Pierre and Jacques.

The only descriptive distinctions among this peasantry concerned their occupations, like Pierre the swineherd or Jacques the ferryman.

The Normans themselves were originally
Vikings (or Northmen) who raided, colonised
and eventually settled down around the French
coastline.

They had sailed up the Seine in their
longboats in 900AD under their ferocious leader
Rollo and ruled the roost in north east France
before sailing over to conquer England, bringing
their relatively new tradition of having surnames
with them.

It took another hundred years for the
Normans to percolate northwards and surnames
did not begin to appear in Scotland until the
thirteenth century.

These adventurous knights brought an
aura of chivalry with them and it was said no
damsel of any distinction would marry a man
unless he had at least two names.

The family names included that of
Scotland's great hero Robert De Brus and his
compatriots were warriors from families like the
De Morevils, De Umphravils, De Berkelais,
De Quincis, De Viponts and De Vaux.

As the knights settled the boundaries of their vast estates, they took territorial names, as in Hamilton, Moray, Crawford, Cunningham, Dunbar, Ross, Wemyss, Dundas, Galloway, Renfrew, Greenhill, Hazelwood, Sandylands and Church-hill.

Other names, though not with any obvious geographical or topographical features, nevertheless derived from ancient parishes like Douglas, Forbes, Dalyell and Guthrie.

Other surnames were coined in connection with occupations, castles or legendary deeds.

Stuart originated in the word steward, a prestigious post which was an integral part of any large medieval household. The same applied to Cooks, Chamberlains, Constables and Porters.

Borders towns and forts – needed in areas like the Debateable Lands which were constantly fought over by feuding local families – had their own distinctive names; and it was often from them that the resident groups took their communal titles, as in the Grahams of Annandale, the Elliots and Armstrongs of the East Marches, the Scotts and Kerrs of Teviotdale and Eskdale.

Even physical attributes crept into surnames, as in Small, Little and More (the latter being 'beg' in Gaelic), Long or Lang, Stark, Stout, Strong or Strang and even Jolly.

Mieklejohns would have had the strength of several men, while Littlejohn was named after the legendary sidekick of Robin Hood.

Colours got into the act with Black, White, Grey, Brown and Green (Red developed into Reid, Ruddy or Ruddiman). Blue was rare and nobody ever wanted to be associated with yellow.

Pompous worthies took the name Wiseman, Goodman and Goodall.

Words intimating the sons of leading figures were soon affiliated into the language as in Johnson, Adamson, Richardson and Thomson, while the Norman equivalent of Fitz (from the French-Latin 'filius' meaning 'son') cropped up in Fitzmaurice and Fitzgerald.

The prefix 'Mac' was 'son of' in Gaelic and clans often originated with occupations – as in

MacNab being sons of the Abbot, MacPherson and MacVicar being sons of the minister and MacIntosh being sons of the chief.

The church's influence could be found in the names Kirk, Clerk, Clarke, Bishop, Friar and Monk. Proctor came from a church official, Singer and Sangster from choristers, Gilchrist and Gillies from Christ's servant, Mitchell, Gilmory and Gilmour from servants of St Michael and Mary, Malcolm from a servant of Columba and Gillespie from a bishop's servant.

The rudimentary medical profession was represented by Barber (a trade which also once included dentistry and surgery) as well as Leech or Leitch.

Businessmen produced Merchants, Mercers, Monypennies, Chapmans, Sellers and Scales, while down at the old village watermill the names that cropped up included Miller, Walker and Fuller.

Other self explanatory trades included Coopers, Brands, Barkers, Tanners, Skinners, Brewsters and Brewers, Tailors, Saddlers, Wrights,

Cartwrights, Smiths, Harpers, Joiners, Sawyers, Masons and Plumbers.

Even the scenery was utilised as in Craig, Moor, Hill, Glen, Wood and Forrest.

Rank, whether high or low, took its place with Laird, Barron, Knight, Tennant, Farmer, Husband, Granger, Grieve, Shepherd, Shearer and Fletcher.

The hunt and the chase supplied Hunter, Falconer, Fowler, Fox, Forrester, Archer and Spearman.

The renowned medieval historian Froissart, who eulogised about the romantic deeds of chivalry (and who condemned Scotland as being a poverty stricken wasteland), once sniffily dismissed the peasantry of his native France as the jacquerie (or the jacques-without-names) but it was these same humble folk who ended up overthrowing the arrogant aristocracy.

In the olden days, only the blueblooded knights of antiquity were entitled to full, proper names, both Christian and surnames, but with the passing of time and a more egalitarian, less feudal atmosphere, more respectful and worthy titles spread throughout the populace as a whole.

Echoes of a far distant past can still be found in most names and they can be borne with pride in commemoration of past generations who fought and toiled in some capacity or other to make our nation what it now is, for good or ill.

Chapter two:

The sons of Thomas

One of the most common surnames in the United Kingdom, 'Thomson' is the commonest form of spelling found in Scotland, while 'Thompson' is prevalent in the north of England and 'Thomas' in Wales.

It is a name that does not have any single point of origin, and numerous variants are found throughout Europe and North America, including Thom, Thomsoun, Thomason, and Thomsen.

A family of Thomsons, or 'sons of Thom, or Tom', is known to have possessed the estate of what is now the present day Edinburgh suburb of Duddingston for several centuries until it was sold at the close of the seventeenth century, while a family of Thomsons who boasted their own heraldic arms and motto of 'Truth will prevail' held what is now the Edinburgh suburb of Corstorphine.

One of the earliest recorded Thomsons in Scotland is a John Thomson of Ayrshire, and it is this Thomson who is the first of the name to enter the nation's turbulent historical record.

Ayrshire was one of the main recruiting grounds for the cause of the great freedom fighter William Wallace and the warrior king Robert the Bruce.

Both heroes had strong family connections with the area, and many of the common folk who hailed from there fought and died in the many campaigns waged over its soil to oust the occupying English garrisons.

Many of these Ayrshire folk were also part of the army that fought beside Bruce at the decisive battle of Bannockburn in 1314, when a highly disciplined and motivated band of Scottish patriots inflicted an overwhelming defeat on the cream of English chivalry.

Little is known of 'John Thomson of Ayr'. But it is reasonable to assume that he fought at Bannockburn with such skill that it was for this reason that Bruce's brother, Edward, selected Thomson to accompany him on his invasion of Ireland.

That John Thomson was no mere foot

soldier in the ranks of Edward Bruce's army is borne out by the fact that he was personally selected by his commander to lead part of the Scottish contingent that sailed from Ayr in May of 1315 in a fleet of 300 galleys.

Landing on the coast of Antrim, Edward quickly rallied fellow Celtic support in his daring bid to defeat the occupying Anglo-Irish forces that owed allegiance to Edward II of England.

Edward Bruce was recognised as king of Ireland by the anti-English Gaels of Ireland, and a series of stunning victories ensued over the first initial months of the campaign, including the capture of both Carrickfergus and Dundalk.

The Anglo-Irish forces rallied, however, and the next three years were marked with a bloody series of advances and reversals for Bruce until, in 1318, he was killed in a battle fought at Fochart, near Dundalk.

Some sources assert his defeat was caused by his headstrong and impetuous refusal to wait for the arrival of reinforcements before engaging in battle.

The fate of John Thomson is unclear, but it is likely that as leader of one of the Scottish contingents he died in the thick of the fierce battle, along with Edward Bruce.

It is to be hoped his body did not suffer the same gruesome fate as Edward's, which was cut up into four quarters and sent to the four main quarters of the island he had invaded three years earlier.

While John Thomson was furthering the cause of the Bruces in attempting to forge a pan-Celtic alliance against the English, other 'Thomsons' were also deeply embedded in Scotland's own Gaelic tradition.

Gaelic equivalents of Thomson are found in MacTavish ('son of Tammas'), McCombie ('son of Tommy'), and MacThomas (or MacComish, meaning 'son of Thomas'), while MacLehose stems from 'Mac gille Thoismis', meaning 'son of St. Thomas.'

An often heated debate that still rages at the present day concerns with which particular clans 'the Thomsons' can claim an affinity, or kinship.

Untangling the highly complex genealogical web, however, it is possible to identify close 'Thomson' links with Clan MacThomas, Clan MacTavish, Clan Campbell of Argyll, and, through Clan Mackintosh, the great confederation of clans known as Clan Chattan.

All these clans figure greatly in Scotland's colourful and often bloody saga, and Thomsons of today who can trace an ancestry back to them can rightly share in their proud traditions and rich heritage.

Chapter three:

A gathering of clans

**A small wooded knoll marks all that remains
of the MacThomson lands in Glenshee.
Situated about four miles south of the Spitall
of Glenshee and off the Blairgowrie to
Braemar road, it survives today as the
traditional Gathering Place of the clan.**

The history of the MacThomases is
inextricably linked with that of the Mackintoshes,
who were the predominant clan in the great Clan
Chattan confederation.

This mighty confederation also included
MacPhersons, Farquharsons, McBains, MacLeans,
McGillivrays, and Davidsons.

'Touch not the cat without a glove' is the
Clan Chattan motto, while a rampant wildcat is
the crest of this clan that flourished for centuries
in the Badenoch region of the Spey Valley.

Adam MacWilliam of Garvamore,
recognised as the Mackintosh ancestor of Clan

MacThomas, was a son of the 7th Chief of Clan Mackintosh.

A descendant of his, known as MacThomaidh ('Big Tommy'), is thought to have taken his followers from Badenoch into Glenshee, in Perthshire, and by the middle of the sixteenth century a MacThomas clan chief had been confirmed in the lands of Finegand.

A Clan MacThomas 'in Gleneschie' (Glenshee) is listed in the Roll of Clans in both 1587 and 1594, but their fortunes rapidly declined following their support of the Marquis of Montrose and, later, their collaboration with the Cromwellian occupation of Scotland.

A bitter civil war raged in Scotland between 1638 and 1649 between the forces of those Presbyterian Scots who had signed a National Covenant that opposed the divine right of the Stuart monarchy and Royalists such as James Graham, 1st Marquis of Montrose, whose prime allegiance was to Charles I.

Although Montrose had initially supported the Covenant, his conscience later forced him to switch sides, and the MacThomases supported him during his great campaigns from 1644 to 1645, a year that became known as the Year of Miracles because of his brilliant military successes.

These campaigns included the Battle of Inverlochy, fought and won by Montrose in February of 1645 after he and his hardy band of followers, that included MacThomases, had endured a gruelling 36-hour march south through knee-deep snow from the area of the present day Fort Augustus to Inverlochy.

The forces of the Presbyterian Earl of Argyll were wiped out in a surprise attack and the earl himself forced to flee.

The MacThomases also shared in Montrose's great victory at Kilsyth on August 15, 1645, but also shared in his final defeat at Philiphaugh, near Selkirk, less than a month later.

Charles I met his grim end on the executioner's block in January of 1649, and it was just over a year later, in June of 1650, that Oliver Cromwell, as Lord General of the Commonwealth Forces of England, crossed the

Tweed into Scotland at the head of a 16,000-strong force of seasoned cavalry and deadly artillery.

He entered a war-ravaged nation that was bitterly divided along religious and political lines.

Charles II would later be crowned king at Scone, but only because he had, reluctantly, agreed to sign both the National Covenant and the Solemn League and Covenant, the sentiments of which were so precious to Scotland's dominant and fanatical Presbyterian faction.

The Scots army was routed by Cromwell at the Battle of Dunbar on September 3, 1650, with up to 3,000 Scots killed and nearly 10,000 taken prisoner, with the remainder, commanded by General David Leslie, fleeing north to Perth.

A victorious Cromwell entered Edinburgh on September 7, marking the beginning of the long occupation of Scotland by his troops.

The occupation brought much needed stability to a Scotland that had been torn apart by civil war, and it was in recognition of this that clan chiefs such as the Chief of Clan MacThomas collaborated with Cromwell, seeing this as serving not only their own interests but the interests of the nation as a whole.

The MacThomases paid dearly for their co-operation with Cromwell's republican regime, when in 1660, following the restoration of Charles II to the throne, they fell out of favour.

Clans that had remained faithful to the royal cause were duly rewarded, often at the expense of clans such as the MacThomases.

Their fortunes rapidly declined, and displaced MacThomas clansmen moved from their ancient ancestral homelands to settle in the Lowlands, in many cases reluctantly changing their name to Thomson or Thomas to disassociate them from a name that was viewed with suspicion by the authorities.

A Clan MacThomas Society flourishes today and takes as its motto 'With God's help, I will overcome envy', while its crest is a rampant wildcat clutching a serpent.

Thomsons can also claim kinship with the proud clan of MacTavish ('son of Tammas') who along with other clans thrived in the vast territory of Argyll, which was dominated for centuries by the Campbells.

This connection with the Campbells explains how some sources assert that the Thomsons are actually a sept of the Campbells of Argyll. The Campbells of Argyll, who claim descent from early Irish kings, have, as their motto 'Forget not', while their crest is a boar's head.

The MacTavish crest also features a boar's head, and the motto of this clan that adhered to the Jacobite cause is 'Do not forget me after death.'

A contentious issue in recent years is whether or not Clan MacTavish can claim all Thomsons or Thompsons as clansmen.

Any Thomsons or Thompsons, however, who can trace an ancestry back to the MacTavish lands of Dunardary, near the western end of the Crinan canal in Argyll, or the areas of Kilberry, Knapdale, and Kilmichael Glassary, may well in all probability be descendants of the original 'sons of Tammas' of Argyll.

A mystery surrounds a faded parchment still held today by the office of the Lord Lyon King of Arms of Scotland and known as Workman's Manuscript.

Dated to 1665-66, the document attributes arms to an unnamed 'Thomson of that Ilk', while over the centuries arms have been granted as 'indeterminate cadets', or branches of the 'honoured community' of Thomsons, to Thomsons who have petitioned the Lord Lyon.

Further complicating the tangled genealogical strands, bearers of the name Thomason have links with Clan MacFarlane, and are thought to descend from Thomas, the son of a late fourteenth and early fifteenth century MacFarlane chief.

During the bloody early seventeenth century campaign by James VI to bring much needed law and order to the Highlands and Islands, the MacFarlanes were among some of the particularly unruly clans that suffered the dire penalty of being proscribed and having their lands, between Arrochar on Loch Long and

Tarbet on Loch Lomond, forfeited. The clan had also held lands around Loch Sloy.

Forced to move to other parts of Scotland, many MacFarlanes had no option but to change their name, in many cases to Thomason.

The MacFarlane motto is "This I'll defend", while the crest is a demi-savage brandishing a broadsword pointing to an imperial crown.

Chapter four:

On the world stage

Thomsons, and those bearing variants of the spelling of the name, have stamped a significant mark on the international stage in a range of activities ranging from the sciences and architecture to the arts and the world of publishing.

Born in Belfast in 1824 but moving to Scotland when he was aged eight, William Thomson is better known as the pioneering mathematician and physicist Lord Kelvin.

Immersing himself at Glasgow University in the study of astronomy, chemistry, and natural philosophy (as physics was then known), Thomson was aged only 15 when he was awarded a university gold medal for one of his essays.

Pursuing further studies at Cambridge University, he returned to Scotland after being elected to the chair of natural philosophy at Glasgow University.

His study of thermodynamics led him in 1848 to propose an absolute scale of temperature, used by scientists today and known as the Kelvin.

His work on the first successful telegraph transmissions by the transatlantic cable between Ireland and Newfoundland, and his contributions to electrical science, led to him being elevated to the peerage as 1st Baron Kelvin of Largs in 1866.

The 'Kelvin' in the title refers to the river that runs through the grounds of Glasgow University, while Largs is the Scottish west coast resort where he built his home, and died in 1907.

The Scottish zoologist Sir D'Arcy Wentworth Thompson, who was born in 1860 and died in 1948, was the author of the landmark *On Growth and Form*, recognised as having exerted a major influence on biological science, while English physicist Sir George Paget Thomson, who was born in 1892 and died in 1975, won a Nobel Prize for his work in 1937.

Another Nobel Prize winner was the English physicist and mathematician Sir Joseph Thomson, who led a group of researchers at

Cambridge University's famed Cavendish laboratory.

He was the first to establish that cathode rays were moving particles whose speed and specific charge could be measured.

Born in Stonehaven, in the northeast of Scotland, in 1822, Robert William Thomson not only patented the fountain pen, but was also the original inventor of the vulcanised rubber pneumatic tyre.

Patented in 1845, it was considered too expensive, however, and it was left to fellow Scot John Dunlop to 're-invent' and refine Thomson's original idea, more than 40 years later.

Born in London in 1770, David Thompson is recognised as one of the world's greatest geographers. Despite the disadvantage of being born blind in one eye, he explored and mapped northwest Canada.

In the world of the arts, James Thomson, born in 1700 and who died in 1748, was the Scottish poet who wrote the critically acclaimed *The Seasons* and *The Castle of Indolence*, while

Glasgow-born poet and essayist James Thomson (1834-82) penned *The City of Dreadful Night*.

In more recent times, the gifted Welsh poet Dylan Thomas ('Thomas' being the most common form of 'Thomson' in Wales), who was born in 1914 and died in 1953, is remembered for a series of poems he wrote in his short lifetime, particularly *Under Milk Wood*.

A pioneer in the 20th century of what has become known as 'The New Journalism', American-born Hunter S. Thompson popularised the 'first person' style of journalism, and was author of a range of works that include *Fear and Loathing in Las Vegas* and *The Great Shark Hunt*.

He died in February of 2005, aged 67, from self-inflicted gunshot wounds.

Born in Balfron, Stirlingshire, in 1817, Alexander Thomson is better known as 'Greek' Thomson for his unique style of architecture, many examples of which are still to be seen in Glasgow and surrounding areas.

His diverse style included Greek, Indian, and Egyptian influences, while he also pioneered what were then 'modern' materials such as plate-glass and cast-iron. He died in 1875.

In the world of publishing, Roy Thomson was the Canadian-born barber's son of Scots descent who died in 1976, aged 82, as a multi-millionaire and owner of an extensive range of newspaper, radio, and television interests throughout the world.

He became Lord Thomson of Fleet after being raised to the peerage in 1964 as 1st Baron of Fleet, the 'Fleet' referring to London's Fleet Street, which until recent times was the publishing centre of many of Britain's best-selling newspapers.

Dundee-based D.C. Thomson and Co. Ltd, publishers of a hugely popular range of newspapers, magazines, and children's comics and comic books, has been a dominant force in the publishing world for many years.

In the world of sport, John Thomson was a talented Glasgow Celtic Football Club goalkeeper from the coalmining village of Cardenden, in Fife.

His promising career was tragically cut short at the age of 22 when he died after sustaining a head injury in an accidental clash with a rival Rangers player in a match played on September 5, 1931.

More than 30,000 mourners attended his funeral, and his memory lives on today in the haunting *Ballad of Johnny Thomson*.

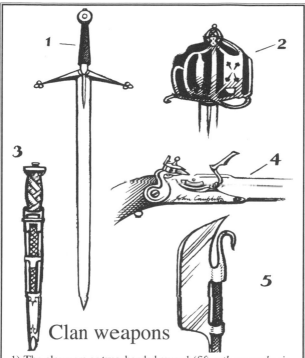

Clan weapons

1) The claymore or two-handed sword *(fifteenth or early six-teenth century)*
2) Basket hilt of broadsword made in Stirling, 1716
3) Highland dirk *(eighteenth century)*
4) Steel pistol *(detail)* made in Doune
5) Head of Lochaber Axe as carried in the '45 and earlier